Louisa May Alcott

YOUNG WRITER

by Laurence Santrey
illustrated by Sandra Speidel

Troll Associates

Library of Congress Cataloging in Publication Data

Santrey, Laurence.
    Louisa May Alcott, young writer.

    Summary: A biography of an early American writer,
whose own life was reflected in her famous novels,
such as "Little Women" and "Little Men."
    1. Alcott, Louisa May, 1832-1888—Biography—
Juvenile literature. 2. Authors, American—19th century—
Biography—Juvenile literature. [1. Alcott, Louisa May,
1832-1888. 2. Authors, American] I. Speidel, Sandra,
ill. II. Title.
PS1018.S19   1986   813'.4 [B] [92]   85-1086
ISBN 0-8167-0563-1 (lib. bdg.)
ISBN 0-8167-0564-X (pbk.)

Louisa May Alcott

YOUNG WRITER

Little Louisa stood by the fireplace, telling her family a new story she had thought of all by herself. Louisa's parents and her sisters were a perfect audience. They listened closely to her. All of them loved Louisa's stories, which were full of interesting people and exciting adventures.

Yet no one in the house that evening could have known that this young girl would one day grow up to be a famous writer. Today, over one hundred years later, Louisa May Alcott's books are still read and loved by millions of readers. It was Louisa's memories of growing up, of her unusual family, and of good times and bad, that she brought to life in her most famous book, *Little Women*.

Louisa May Alcott was born in Germantown, Pennsylvania, on November 29, 1832. She was the second child of Bronson and Abigail May Alcott. Her big sister, Anna, was a year and a half older. Mr. and Mrs. Alcott were from New England, but Mr. Alcott's work as a school teacher had brought them to Germantown, a small town near Philadelphia. Bronson Alcott had been offered a fine opportunity to teach in a new private school that had been built in Germantown. There, Alcott hoped to express all his ideas about life, children, and education.

Bronson Alcott believed that all children, boys *and* girls, deserved to be educated. He believed that children should be treated with as much respect as grownups. He believed their opinions were important.

Bronson Alcott's ideas may not seem strange today. But in the nineteenth century these ideas were revolutionary. When the parents of his pupils in Germantown found out about Mr.

Alcott's teaching ideas, they took their children
out of the school. Soon after, the school was
closed for good.

Now life became difficult for the Alcotts. Mr. Alcott was not making enough money to feed his two little children or to pay the rent for their home. To earn money, Mr. Alcott opened a small school in Philadelphia. This meant he had to be away from his family all week. It made everyone sad, but they had no choice.

Mrs. Alcott, called "Marmee" by her daughters, had to face many problems and worries. Her husband was a wonderful, idealistic man. However, he was not successful at making a living. Throughout his life, Mr. Alcott would fail at one thing after another, while his wife carried the burden of keeping home and family together.

No matter how she felt inside, Marmee did her best to be cheerful and calm. She told the children that money and possessions really didn't matter. She said that love, family closeness, and doing the right things were what counted most.

Marmee taught her girls to find joy in whatever life offered them. It might be baking a pie, having a snowball fight, or reading by firelight in the evening. Even on the gloomiest days, there was warmth in the Alcott household. It was this feeling of security and love that Louisa remembered most and wrote about in her books.

When Mr. Alcott's Philadelphia school failed,
the family moved back to Massachusetts. Their
new home was a house near a big park in Boston

called the Common. Close by, on Temple Place, Mr. Alcott opened another school. It was named the Temple School and started with thirty students. They came from some of the best families in Boston.

The great writer and philosopher Ralph Waldo Emerson, and other important New Englanders, believed that Bronson Alcott was a genius and a brilliant teacher. That was the highest praise any teacher could receive. The support of these important people should have made the Temple School a success.

But even with this marvelous start, the school was doomed. Bronson Alcott taught his pupils how to think. He felt it was important for each student to search for and discover life's meaning. However, this left little time for reading, writing, and arithmetic. As in Philadelphia, parents soon took their children out of the school, and it was closed.

By now there were three Alcott children to feed. The third daughter, Elizabeth, had been born in 1835. It was harder than ever for the Alcotts to buy food and clothing for the family. But Louisa and her sisters didn't suffer. Marmee was there, and she always had time to hug them, calm their fears, and kiss away their hurts.

As for their father, Louisa and her sisters felt that he was the smartest person in the world. He answered all their questions. He read to them and taught them. Best of all, Mr. Alcott treated his girls seriously and with respect.

In Boston, Louisa got to know her mother's family, the Mays. That was fun for the little girl. Marmee's relations didn't do things the way the Alcotts did. The Mays were quite prim and proper. Even so, they were kind, likable people, and Louisa looked forward to seeing them.

Louisa's favorite relative was Aunt Hancock. Aunt Hancock was the model for the character of Aunt March in *Little Women*. Her real name was Mrs. Dorothy Scott. But before she married James Scott, she had been married to John Hancock. He was one of the signers of the Declaration of Independence and was the first governor of Massachusetts.

Aunt Hancock was so proud to have been married to John Hancock that she kept his name until the day she died. She was a strong-willed woman with an opinion on everything. Louisa loved hearing family stories about Aunt Hancock.

After the Temple School closed, the Alcotts rented a home in nearby Concord, Massachusetts. It was a confusing time for Louisa and her sisters. Another baby had been born, a boy, but he died soon after. This made the Alcotts very sad. But moving into their new house was like starting a new life. Soon the gloom and confusion became part of the past.

Hosmer Cottage was the name of their Concord home. It was a small house, but it had gardens, fields, pine woods, and a river close by. Louisa delighted in the freedom of running through the meadows, exploring the quiet woods, and listening to the birds.

Louisa was an active, high-spirited child. She always loved to roam on her own. That had been a problem in Boston, with its busy streets. But Concord was a dream-come-true for her. It was also a relief for Marmee. At last, she didn't have to worry about where her busy little girl might have wandered.

In Concord, Bronson Alcott took whatever work was offered to him. He did gardening and farming, whenever a neighbor hired him. But mostly Mr. Alcott earned a small living as a woodchopper.

Louisa and her sisters had no idea of how poor

they had become. The Alcotts ate the same simple food they had always eaten, because they were followers of Sylvester Graham. People today remember him as the man who created the graham cracker. Back then, Sylvester Graham was famous for his ideas about nutrition and health.

Graham believed that good health came from taking cold showers, sleeping on hard mattresses, getting lots of fresh air, and always being happy at mealtime. He was against eating sugar, meat, and butter, and drinking coffee and tea. As followers of Graham, the Alcotts ate rice, potatoes, fruits, nuts, and natural grains. They drank water and milk. Whenever they could afford to, they ate chicken or fish.

Today, Graham's diet sounds fairly sensible. But one hundred and fifty years ago, most people thought it was strange. This opinion didn't bother the Alcotts and their friends. They thought for themselves. If a way of life made sense to them, they had the courage to live that way.

This attitude did much to shape Louisa's character. Another important idea of Papa Alcott's was that learning should be fun. The school Louisa would write about in a book called *Little Men* was a merry, lively place. It wasn't at all like most real schools in those days. It was like Papa's ideal school. Louisa's fictional schoolmaster, Mr. Bhaer, is a lot like her father.

Bronson Alcott had a witty method for teaching his daughters the alphabet. He acted out each letter with his body. For the letter "I," he stood very straight. For the letter "X," he stretched his arms and legs in four different directions. Louisa's favorite was Papa doing the letter "S." He twisted his body and arms and neck until he was as close to an "S" as possible. At the same time, he imitated the hissing of a goose. That taught the girls the sound of an "S" as well as the shape. It never failed to send Louisa into fits of giggles.

Papa also led the family's weekly pillow fight. Every Saturday night, Anna, Louisa, and Elizabeth could hardly wait for bedtime. Papa usually pretended he had forgotten what day it was. But that was part of the fun. Sooner or later, just when the girls couldn't wait another minute, Mr. Alcott went into action. Then *thump!* With pillows flying, shrieks of laughter filled the house.

Everybody in the family except the new baby, named May, joined in. The fun-filled battle didn't end until Papa retreated from the attack of his three pillow-swinging daughters. Exhausted at last, the trio went off to bed.

It was while the Alcotts lived at Hosmer Cottage that Louisa began to write. At eight and a half, she was fascinated by the beauty around her as the seasons changed. As winter gave way to spring, Louisa wrote a poem called, "To the First Robin." It went:

Welcome, welcome, little stranger,
Fear no harm, and fear no danger.
We are glad to see you here,
For you sing, 'Sweet Spring is near.'
Now the white snow melts away;
Now the flowers blossom gay;
Come dear bird and build your nest,
For we love our robin best.

Young Louisa made up dozens of little poems and stories. Her imagination was like a magic carpet. It took her to worlds of adventure and excitement. And it was a perfect way of escaping from the family's money problems. Because there was never enough money, the Alcotts ate only two small meals a day. And what's more, good-hearted Mr. Alcott gave away the little money he did earn.

"There are people in need," he would tell the family. "Don't you think we should help them?" And Marmee and the girls always agreed. No one said anything to him about their own needs. Papa was a noble, good human being, but some people said he lived in a world of dreams.

29

Following one of his dreams, Mr. Alcott went to England. He wanted to see the English school called Alcott House. It had been named after him and was run according to his ideas of education. There was another reason for his journey. A group of New England thinkers, including Ralph Waldo Emerson and Henry David Thoreau, wanted news of the latest philosophical ideas in England. And Bronson Alcott seemed to be the best person for the task. That is why Mr. Emerson offered to pay all of Mr. Alcott's costs.

Ten-year-old Louisa and her sisters were proud that Papa had a school named after him. Still, they missed him very much in the six months he was away. Marmee tried her best to fill the house with care, affection, and lightheartedness. But life was often grim and lonely, and there was never enough money, even when Marmee's father helped out.

It was kind of Mr. Emerson to pay for Papa's trip, to pay the Alcotts' rent, and to help them in other ways. But it made Louisa sad that her family had to live on charity. Every day Louisa thought about expenses—the cost of food, of paper to write on, of cloth to sew into dresses. It was a heavy burden for a young child. When her shoes became too small for her growing feet, she felt guilty. And rather than tell Marmee the truth, Louisa would run around barefoot, saying she liked it that way.

It was about this time that young Louisa May Alcott came to a decision about her future. She didn't know what she was going to do when she grew up. One day she thought she would be an actress. The next day she was sure she'd be a writer. And the day after that she imagined herself as an artist. But whatever she would become, Louisa was certain of one thing: she was going to make enough money so that the Alcotts would never have to worry again.

The thing that bothered Louisa most was the hardship her mother had to endure. Marmee always smiled and tried not to complain or let her daughters see her worry. But from early morning till late at night, Marmee worked. She cleaned and cooked and brought buckets filled with water from outdoors. She tended the family vegetable garden, washed and mended the clothing, taught the girls their lessons. And, at night, when her other jobs were done, she earned a few pennies doing sewing for other families.

Young Louisa made a vow to herself. She would devote her life to providing for those she loved. Marmee would not spend her older years struggling and worrying. She would have a warm sitting room, and clothing that wasn't faded or mended again and again.

Anna, Elizabeth, and May would have pretty things to wear. They'd go to dances and parties. They would attend any school they wanted to, learn to play a musical instrument, have a pony to ride. And they would never have to miss a meal.

Louisa was set on having a career in order to help her family. And she was willing to sacrifice to reach that goal. In those days, having a career often meant a woman gave up the possibility of marriage and children. As young as she was, Louisa understood that, and it didn't change her mind.

At last, Papa's long European trip was over. Louisa and her sisters were excited at his homecoming. But their joy was dimmed when they saw he had brought three people from England to live with the Alcotts. The cottage was already too small for the family. But Papa Alcott didn't mind giving up the closeness that the family had always enjoyed. He had found something that was more important to him.

Mr. Alcott and his friends had brought home an idea for a new style of life. They planned to form a commune. In it, everyone would share work and whatever they could produce from the land. Each member of the commune would own no property. They would eat simple meals, live plainly, and strive for perfection.

The commune idea sounded lovely, but it didn't work very well. After just one winter, one of the Englishmen moved out. The other two continued to live with the Alcotts, but they weren't doing their share of the labor.

Marmee and the girls were working harder than ever. Anna was a big help because she was even-tempered and good at household tasks. In fact, she was exactly the person Louisa wrote about as Meg March, the oldest sister in *Little Women.*

Louisa was too impatient and rebellious to do her share of the work very well. She grumbled a lot and only pitched in because it made life a bit easier for Marmee. Elizabeth and May were still too small to do much.

In June 1843, when Louisa was eleven and a half years old, the Alcotts moved into a new communal home. The house, called Fruitlands, was located in Harvard, Massachusetts, about fifteen miles from their old house. Their new home was a two-story farmhouse. It sat in the middle of ninety acres of fields, woods, and orchards of apple, cherry, and peach trees. The downstairs section of the house had a living room, a small dining room, and a kitchen. Louisa's favorite spot was the tiny attic. Here, in the quiet, she could sit alone and write or read.

There was a great deal of work to be done both inside and outside the building. It needed painting and many repairs. The farm land was fertile but it had to be plowed, planted, and harvested. A lot of time, effort, and skill would have to be given for Fruitlands to succeed. But Papa had faith that many others would join them in this pure, simple, natural life. For his sake, the Alcott family hoped Papa was right.

Even so, Louisa did not really enjoy living this way. It was dreary and harsh, especially for a high-spirited, fun-loving, imaginative girl like Louisa. Living the good life, according to the commune's rules, meant more than doing a lot of hard work. It also meant giving up much that brought pleasure.

Every day, the whole group sat down for a conversation about goodness. Actually, it was a time for each one of them to talk about his or her faults. Louisa's worst fault, they all agreed, was that she had a mind of her own. She never stopped rebelling against the endless do's and don'ts at Fruitlands.

Her family's criticism made Louisa unhappy. She tried to express her unhappiness in writing. In one poem, she wrote,

How can I learn to rule myself,
To be the child I should,
Honest and brave, nor ever tire
Of trying to be good?

Life did not get much easier for Louisa when the Fruitlands experiment failed. The Alcotts just couldn't seem to settle down. They moved from one house to another to another. No sooner did Louisa make friends in one place than the family pulled up roots and moved on. She hated leaving their little home in Still River, Massachusetts. That is where the Alcotts moved when they left the house in Harvard.

In Still River, Louisa and Anna went to school with the neighborhood children and loved it. For the first time ever, twelve-year-old Louisa belonged to a group of young people and could behave like a normal youngster. The children played tag and hide-and-seek. They held hoop-rolling contests, climbed trees, and went fishing.

What Louisa enjoyed most were the plays the children staged in the woodshed behind the house. Here, she was queen. She was the best writer of the group, and she loved everything about putting on a play. Her favorite kinds of

plays were adventures in which there was a mean
villain, a brave swashbuckling hero, and a lovely
heroine waiting to be saved.

43

Louisa liked to play the most active roles, so she could speak in a deep, booming voice, jump around, and wave her wooden sword. Anna always played the gentle, sweet damsel in distress. Elizabeth and May took whatever roles were left over, glad to be a part of it all.

But the woodshed and the children's friends were soon left behind. The Alcotts moved back to Concord, to a home called Hillside. They lived there for three and a half years, longer than they had lived anywhere before.

As Louisa entered her teen years, her desire to become a writer grew stronger. She kept a journal and wrote hundreds of poems, stories, and plays. At first, not everything she wrote was good, but the more she wrote the better her work became.

When she was a teen-ager, Louisa also helped support the family. She took in sewing, worked as a teacher, and served as a companion to an aged couple. She never received much pay for what she did, but she wrote about all of these experiences when she was older.

From Concord, the Alcotts moved to Boston, where Marmee became one of the first professional social workers in America. Bronson Alcott began to travel around the country, giving lectures. And Louisa kept on writing.

In September 1851, when she was eighteen, Louisa sold a piece of her writing for the first time. It was a poem entitled, "Sunlight." The next spring, a newspaper paid Louisa $5.00 for a short story. Her professional career had begun at last.

In the years to come, Louisa May Alcott worked as a teacher, a nurse in the Civil War, an editor, and a lecturer. All the while she continued to write. And everything of importance that happened in her real life, as well as the things she imagined, went into her books.

There were Elizabeth's illness and death, Louisa's bout with typhoid fever, Anna's marriage, May's cheerful ways—all these and much more became part of *Little Women, Little Men, Jo's Boys,* and the other wonderful books read by millions of her fans the world over.

Her success, and the pleasure she brought young readers, made Louisa very happy. But her greatest joy was realizing her dream of being able to give her family an easier life. She bought Marmee the beautiful Orchard House, in Concord. She took care of Papa, of Anna's family, of May's daughter, Lulu, and of every other needy relative.

Louisa May Alcott died on March 6, 1888. She was fifty-five years of age. But in her heart she was still the character Jo of *Little Women*— the active, life-loving, young girl who would never grow old.